PASSPORT TO LIFE

JOURNEY TO A POSITIVE MINDSET

COTY MARTIN

Passport To Life:

Journey To A Positive Mindset

Coty Martin, MA, LPC

CM Enterprises

Published and Printed in the USA.

ISBN: 978-0692929070

Cover design by Coty Martin

TABLE OF CONTENTS

Part Two: How To Set Effective Goals

ABOUT THE AUTHOR

COTY'S STORY

I was born and raised in Miami, Florida, a troubled and confused kid headed nowhere fast. At the age of 14 I was challenged with the decision of becoming a man or a statistic. I chose to become a man!

Gifted with natural talents on the football field and the ability to express myself both poetically and musically, I began to set goals that would later direct me toward a positive mindset.

Coming from an unstable childhood, I understood the importance of building and maintaining positive relationships. By the time I graduated from high school, I lived in 22 different homes and went to 10 different schools.

I understood early on that perseverance would be the key to overcoming my adverse background and that failure was never an option.

I used football as a tool for positive growth and music as therapy to overcome each adverse phase of my life. And after only playing one full season of varsity in the 10th grade due to two season-ending injuries in 11th and 12th grade, I was still able to successfully graduate high school and earned a full scholarship to play football at South Carolina State University.

After struggling with the transition from high school to college, my "at risk" past presented itself. I was kicked off the football team multiple times due to negative actions off the field and was at risk of losing my scholarship. I then had another season-ending injury that would set me back. I was also in a terrible car accident that caused a serious back injury. Doctors explained to me that I might not be able to play football again, which terrified me.

I immediately turned to my favorite source of therapy, which was music. After months of rehabilitating my injuries and reflecting on my life through recording music, I understood that the only way to overcome adverse situations and succeed was to change my mindset and to do things differently.

After my mindset shift, I would later become the starting running back on the football team, be awarded with multiple Most Valuable Player trophies, All-Conference, and selected to the HBCU All-Star football game where I won Most Valuable Player.

I would later earn my Bachelors and Masters Degrees from South Carolina State University, become a Licensed Professional Counselor and develop a passion for assisting others to embrace and overcome adversity so that they could create a positive mindset for a successful life.

INTRODUCTION

MOVING FORWARD

Life is a journey... and would not be without multiple destinations and pit stops along the way. Some of these waysides are more pleasurable than others, but the key to moving forward in life, which is our ultimate goal, is to distill the good out of our positive as well as not-so positive experiences.

Therefore, we should always keep a positive mindset and never focus on the negative. Focusing on the negative will only lead to moods that will alter our positive thinking temporarily or maybe even permanently. This is certainly easier said than done, but we must focus, at least, on trying. Focusing on the negative will cause us to display moods and emotions such as anger, frustration, sadness, jealousy, envy, hatred, etc. These destructive emotions will not help us move forward.

When focusing on the positive aspects of life's experiences, we will often minimize the negative, perhaps even to the point that it becomes nonexistent. Even better, when we focus on the positive, it naturally causes us to feel and display moods and emotions such as happiness, joy, love, empathy, sympathy, caring, etc., which are helpful in achieving your goals. Again, at the very minimum, we should and must believe it's possible for us to move forward.

With work and constant effort, we can create the life we want to live by constantly motivating ourselves, managing our emotions and setting realistic goals to accomplish, in both short term and long term.

This *Passport To Life* is a personal guide centered around and designed to motivate, inspire and guide you into positive thinking and living habits. *Passport To Life* acts as a "counselor or life coach in your pocket," allowing you to process who you are, who you want to be, as well as providing you with the tools to help you plan your actions step by step. Your "plan of action" allows you to structure your thoughts, set your goals, as well as meet deadlines to reach your goals. You will eliminate racing thoughts and vain attempts at getting to the next phase of life. There's no need to look further: the answers to your questions are here!

This book is divided into three sections. The first section, *Motivation, Inspiration and Guidance* consists of 27 Reflections, which will lay the foundation for creating a positive mindset. Each Reflection focuses on the process of taking a negative and turning it into a positive, using a three-step process:

1. *Recognizing* Negative Feelings and Actions
2. *Sourcing* Positive Thoughts and Understanding
3. *Becoming* Self-Motivated and Encouraging of Self and Others

The result is a more peaceful life for yourself and those around you, which is conducive for personal growth, achievement and success.

The second section, *How To Set Effective Goals*, shows you the process of how to set a goal based on a certain set of conditions (S.M.A.R.T.) and plan actions to meet that goal.

The third section, *Action Plan (Goal Setting)*, consists of templates for making goals that will help you keep track of your progress and create a habit of focusing on taking action within a certain timeframe.

I hope that you will make use of this book and treat it as a guide to creating the life you always wanted.

Coty Martin, MA, LPC

PART ONE:

MOTIVATION, INSPIRATION AND GUIDANCE

27 Reflections

1.

PASSPORT TO LIFE

BE DETERMINED

2017

JOURNEY TO A POSITIVE MINDSET

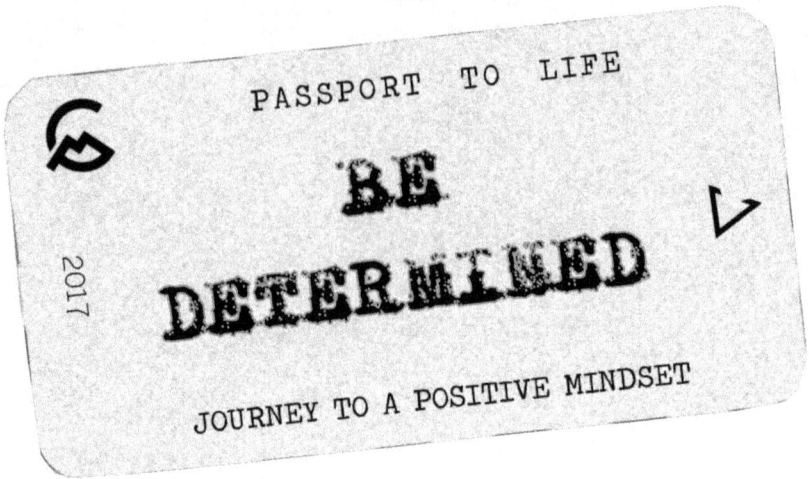

When God is on your side, nothing else matters!

Just know that whatever you are going through will always get better if you have life!

Remember, someone is always doing worse than you are.

The GAME of life is a CHALLENGE, the only way to FAIL is if you QUIT!!!

BE DETERMINED

Sometimes I wake up in the morning with feelings of frustration and fear even though I know that I should be smiling and thankful for all that I have in my life. I have been let down by so many people and situations to the point that my trust is minimal and my faith is weak.

Since I am not unique in this, it is normal to feel this way upon awakening, which makes it important to get into the habit of taking time to center yourself. If you do, your TRUE self will emerge, absent of these negative, unproductive feelings. Many people don't bother with this and so they're stuck with their negativity all through the day.

So, as I take a step back from my selfish thoughts and feelings, I conclude that I do not have it as bad as others may have it. Most importantly, I have life and the ability to change my situation with each day that I am blessed to be on this earth.

There are millions of people who are not physically, mentally or emotionally able to make their situation better and wish that they had the opportunity to do so. There are just as many people who have the opportunity but let it pass them by. I might not be in the situation that I want to be in, but I know that I am in the situation that I *need* to be in so that I can learn what I need to learn.

Therefore, with this determination, I choose to be selfless and not give up on the people who care about me, the people who are depending on me, and the people who are rooting for me to succeed and reach my fullest potential.

Challenges and obstacles are simply a part of life and what matters is how you deal with them. This will decide and define your true character.

God never said that the road to success would be a smooth one, he just promised to get me to my destination safely. I must make the decision to move forward daily.

2.

PASSPORT TO LIFE

FULLFILL
YOUR DREAMS

JOURNEY TO A POSITIVE MINDSET

2017

Don't downgrade your dreams to match your reality, upgrade your faith to match your vision!

Stop seeking validation from others so that you are comfortable achieving YOUR dreams. They are *YOUR* dreams after all!

Greatness doesn't come from being comfortable. Greatness comes from being CHALLENGED!

I have many talents and gifts as well as a lot of dreams that I want to fulfill. Many of my dreams I have down-played or never even spoken about in fear of what someone else might say about them. Even worse, some of my dreams have been put to the side because of what someone had said about them.

I began to realize that my dreams are *my* dreams and no one could fully understand my dreams the way that I do. Therefore, it doesn't make sense for me to continue to ask the opinions of others to seek validation of my dreams. When I stop doing this, I take ownership of my dreams, and the responsibility of achieving them. Therefore, I can't blame anybody else if they don't come true.

Seeking the opinions/approval of others only leaves you confused, frustrated, aggravated and wishing that you never discussed it with them in the first place. The best way to accomplish your dreams is simply to start working on them.

You do not need permission to become successful and the only thing that beats "a failure" is "a try." If you never try, you can't fail, and if you never fail then you will never know what behaviors to correct and actions to take to accomplish that dream. You can *never* fail at something if you never stop trying.

Know what it is that you want and do whatever it takes to accomplish it.

3.

PASSPORT TO LIFE

BECOME THE SOLUTION

2017

JOURNEY TO A POSITIVE MINDSET

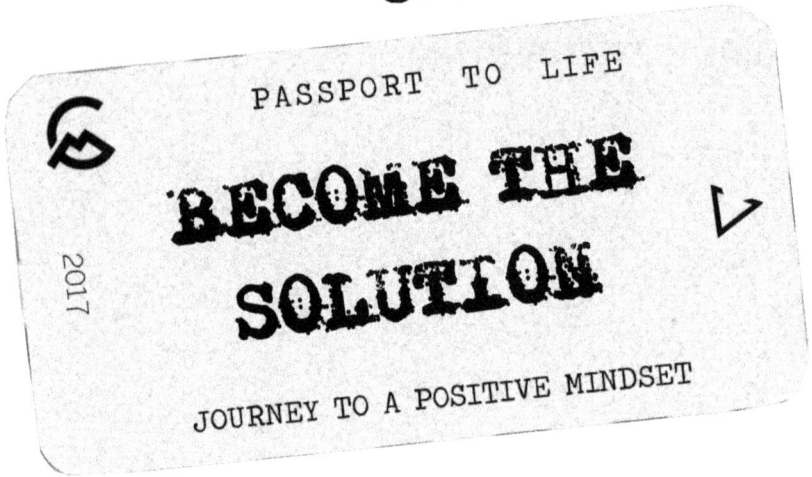

The fight that we need to fight is not physical and driven by HATE, because LOVE conquers ALL.

Loving each other, respecting each other, coming together as a people is the recipe to see CHANGE.

Let's not fuel the flame that is the problem, let's water the plants and watch them grow.

BECOME THE SOLUTION

It is easy to get frustrated, lose your cool and physically harm something or someone. The challenge is, after becoming frustrated, keeping a level head and understanding that the only way to reduce the chance of any further problems is to remain positive.

Most people react out of impulse and emotion, never thinking of the consequences before they act, and it usually doesn't end well.

Taking a minute or two to think about the consequences before acting out can protect you from a potential major life-changing event. Possible life changing events can consist of physical harm, ruining your reputation, expulsion, losing your job, going to jail or even losing your life.

I have learned that respecting others in the manner that you would like to be respected will get you a lot further in life than not doing so. As cliché as it may sound, treating people the way you want to be treated is a basic life rule to live by.

Something as simple as listening to the point of view of others in a conversation and taking some points into consideration before forming your own opinion can prevent arguments/debates and create understanding.

Understanding that positive energy travels and often a simple conversation (whether you agree or disagree) can lead to world-changing events and

/BECOME THE SOLLUTION

create lifelong partnerships.

4.

PASSPORT TO LIFE

CONTROL YOUR HAPPINESS

JOURNEY TO A POSITIVE MINDSET

2017

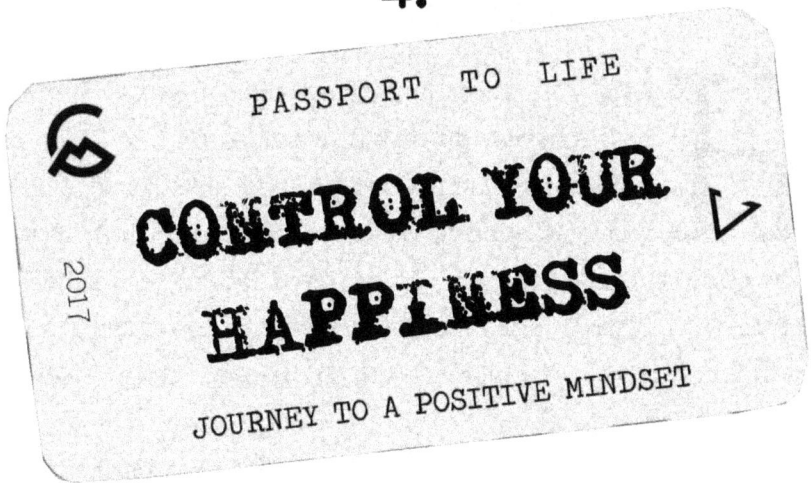

No one is special enough to disrupt your happiness.

Live, Love and Be Happy!

CONTROL YOUR HAPPINESS

Have you ever heard of the phrase "he who angers you controls you" and "the best revenge is living well?" I wish I would have fully understood this concept when I was younger, because I would have avoided a lot of trouble in my life. I used to be quick to react and slow to think. Often, I would react in a way that I would immediately regret.

I used to let anyone or anything upset me (to the point that I would immediately lose my cool) and would not think or care about the consequences. I learned quickly that losing my cool was really about me losing my control. Once you lose control of yourself, the other person or situation can have their way with you and your fate flies out of your hands and into theirs.

Instead of allowing someone else's actions to take you off your path to happiness, allow that person's actions to fuel the flame inside of you that burns with confidence. Think of your peace and happiness as something extremely valuable, maybe even non-transferrable; you certainly wouldn't want to give it away for free, would you?

Be confident enough with yourself to know that you are the prize in any situation you face and that your value does not end with failure, hurt or disappointment.

Failure, hurt and disappointment are a part of life and are to be expected. There are lessons to be learned behind those feelings and emotions. Without them, how would we know what happiness feels like?

5.

PASSPORT TO LIFE

PERSEVERANCE IS THE KEY

2017

JOURNEY TO A POSITIVE MINDSET

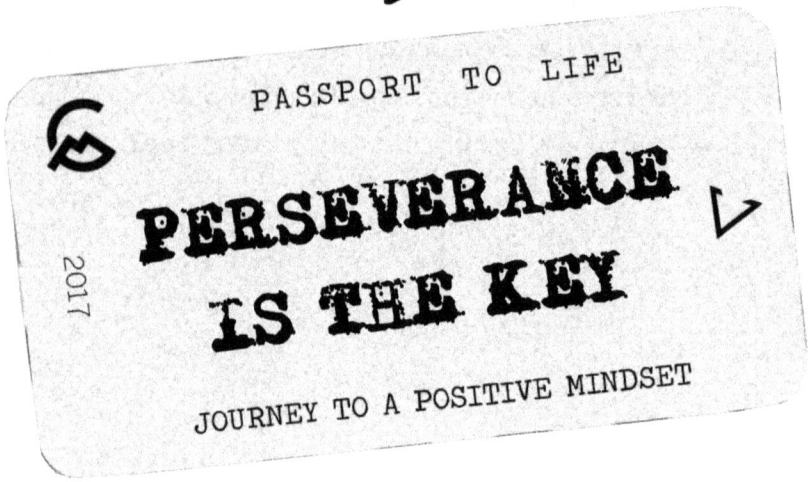

Tough times don't last.
Tough **people** do!

PERSEVERANCE IS THE KEY

I have made a lot of bad decisions in my life, (some worse than others). The pain I caused myself and other people seemed unnecessary, but through acceptance and taking responsibility for my actions, I realized that some good had come from them. In fact, if I hadn't made those mistakes, I wouldn't have become the person I am today.

Every bad decision I made in the past was like taking a life course. Although I failed a lot of those courses starting out, I often made up the grades and ultimately graduated from Adversity University.

I saw that each experience was necessary for my "education" and personal growth. I realize now that if I could re-write my life's story, I wouldn't change anything. I never knew that the decisions I made when I was younger would prepare me for life as much as they did.

I could easily blame my negative life situations on not having a father present or being on my own as a teenager, but ultimately all the bad decisions I made were choices of mine. Every decision I've made in life, either good or bad, was my own and no one else's. Therefore, I had to live with the consequences that resulted.

The one thing that was a constant in every stage of my life was I never gave up! I always persevered through every situation. If I made a bad decision, I spent a lot of time trying to turn that negative into a positive and did a pretty good job at doing so.

The one thing I know about life is, if I continue to wake up and strive to be a better person than I was yesterday, then the good will always outweigh the bad. I lived through the storms (literally and figuratively) and there is only one way to go from here and that is up!

In all that you go through in life, just know that after the storm the sun will soon shine. Cloudy days aren't forever; everything has an expiration date, you just have to be willing to weather the storm.

6.

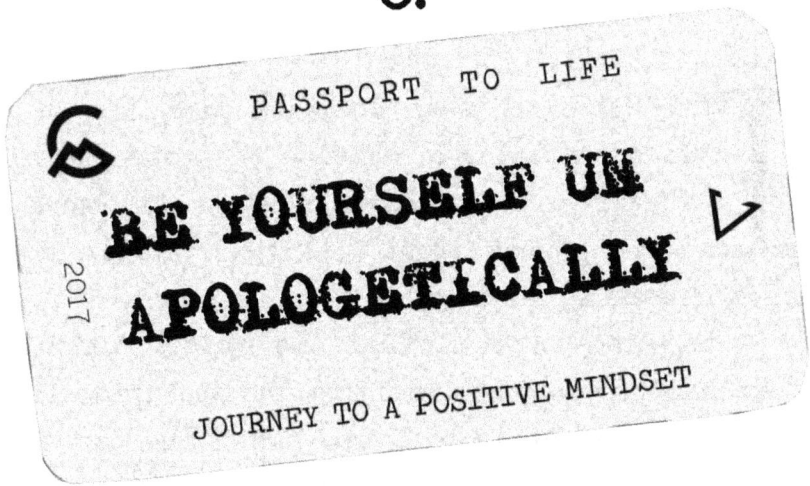

Why fit in when you were born to stand out!?!?

Be who you want to be.

Do what you want to do.

Don't give in to what THEY want you to be and do!

BE YOURSELF UNAPOLOGETICALLY

I t's OK to live an inspired life. It's OK to find something or someone who motivates and inspires you to become a better YOU. There is nothing weak about following your inspiration, wherever it takes you.

It's also OK to follow the rules. Following rules teaches you responsibility and accountability.

What's *not* OK is to think INSIDE the box! True success and achievement come from those who think OUTSIDE the box. You can add your unique perspective and way of thinking to solve problems that more traditional mindsets cannot.

Don't let the way others think, feel and judge define who you are and what you will be. You are unique and you have been put on this earth to leave your unique footprint behind.

If you allow others to dictate your path in life, how will you ever know YOUR purpose?

7.

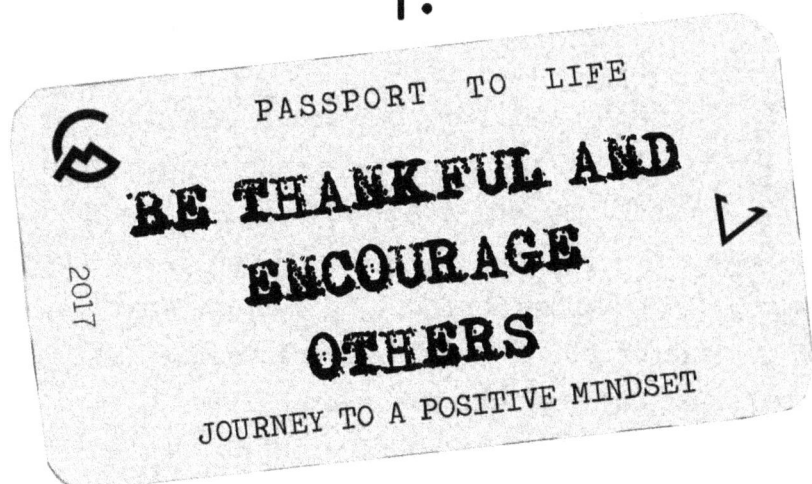

Thank God for waking you and giving you another day on this earth.

Keep a smile on your face, refuse to feel sorry for yourself!

Somebody needs you!

Make at least 10 random compliments today.

Be a blessing to someone!

BE THANKFUL AND ENCOURAGE OTHERS

I used to wake up with a poor attitude for no reason. I didn't smile or even speak to anyone in the house. I used to think I responded this way simply because I was tired. Then I came to the realization that no one did anything to me to make me act this way and there might be much more wrong with me than just being tired.

Waking up in the morning is not a guarantee, but a blessing. So when you wake up in the morning and take your first conscious breath, one of the first things you should do is thank God and pray for those around you.

When you wake up in the morning, there should never be a frown on your face or feelings of anger! Energy travels, so whatever type of energy you give off, you can expect to get it right back.

Challenge yourself to maintain a positive perspective and know that there are people in this world who are dealing with much more serious issues that they cannot just make go away or even improve with simple desire alone.

Carry this positivity with you and share it with others. One way to do that is to compliment those you come in contact with. Not only will it make them feel good, it will prove that you are paying attention to your surroundings and more importantly your interaction with them. You are not just going through life with blinders on. Most times a simple smile or compliment to a random person can be the determining factor of that person losing hope or growing faith.

Never judge anyone, just wish him or her well. Be a blessing!

8.

PASSPORT TO LIFE

BE UNDERSTANDING AND UPLIFT OUR YOUTH

2017

JOURNEY TO A POSITIVE MINDSET

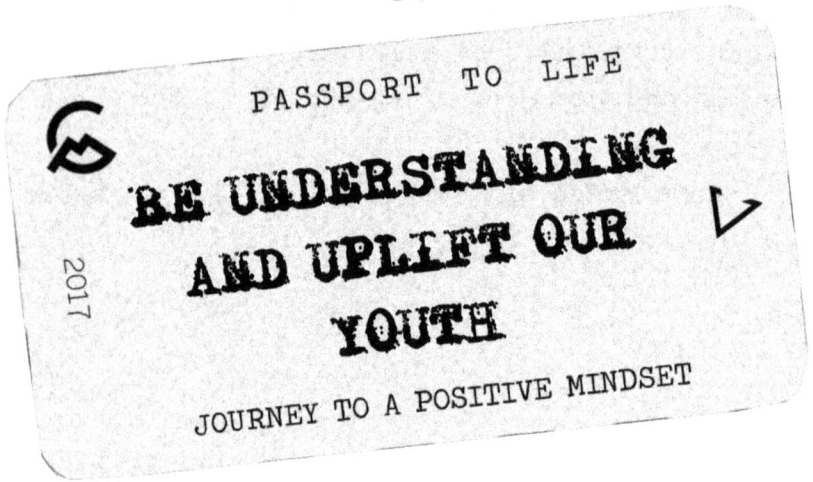

Children did not ask to be here.

We can either discourage our children to bring out the WORST in them!

OR

We can encourage our children to bring out the BEST in them!

BE UNDERSTANDING AND UPLIFT OUR YOUTH

Often we meet, observe and interact with children that we naturally either take a liking or a disliking to. Although most won't admit it, there is some transference blocking you from being empathetic to that child, maybe because the interaction reminds you of something or someone from your past.

You should remind yourself that the child you come in to contact with did not ask to be born into a life situation that would fail to teach them the proper ways of interacting, communicating, behaving, dressing or even speaking. It is not their fault; sometimes it's not even their parent's fault that they are not teaching at home. Parents sometimes just don't know how to teach, because they were never taught themselves. So take time out to understand a situation before forming an opinion on it.

Remember, all behaviors are learned and conditioned behaviors. To judge someone is to see one's self as perfect and no one walking the face of this earth is perfect. It is on you as a human being to motivate, encourage and teach the youth about how to conduct themselves; instead of focusing on the problems that are developing in our youth, we need to focus on the solutions and how to make them better people. We should understand them and meet them where they are to guide them to where they need to be.

9.

PASSPORT TO LIFE

INVEST IN TODAYS YOUTH

2017

JOURNEY TO A POSITIVE MINDSET

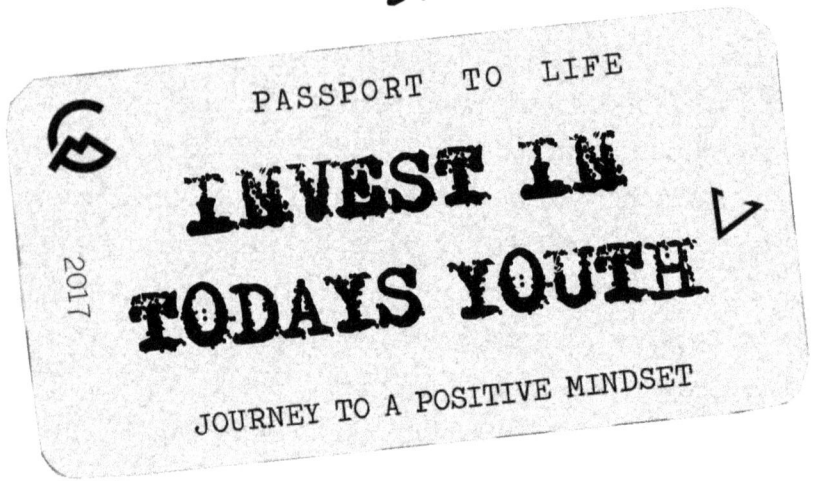

Invest in these children…

Simply looking at them and judging them will not help.

THEY NEED YOU!

Let's all be a part of the SOLUTION and not the problem.

Life is about choices; let's choose to make our communities "GREAT AGAIN!"

INVEST IN TODAY'S YOUTH

Empowerment through experience is the best way to reach our youth. Simply lecturing and telling them what they need to be doing will not spark the fire that needs to be started in the mind of such curious individuals. Action speaks louder than words and exposure feeds curiosity.

Embracing our youth and everything that comes along with them takes character and commitment. If we become part of a child's life, we do not have the luxury of setting them up for failure. We are obligated to prepare them for success. We cannot abandon a child based on a relationship that did not work out in our favor. If you enter a child's life, don't exit for your own personal and selfish reasons. At a certain point, life needs to become less about "you" and more about "youth."

Today's youth are our future and unless we do something to make them believe that, then we are setting them up for failure. Become a blessing in life and allow others to dream and assist our youth in reaching their full potential. It really takes a village to raise our youth up into the people we would want them to be. It's not an overnight task but a lifetime achievement.

10.

PASSPORT TO LIFE

EMBRACE FAILURE AND LEARN FROM IT

JOURNEY TO A POSITIVE MINDSET

2017

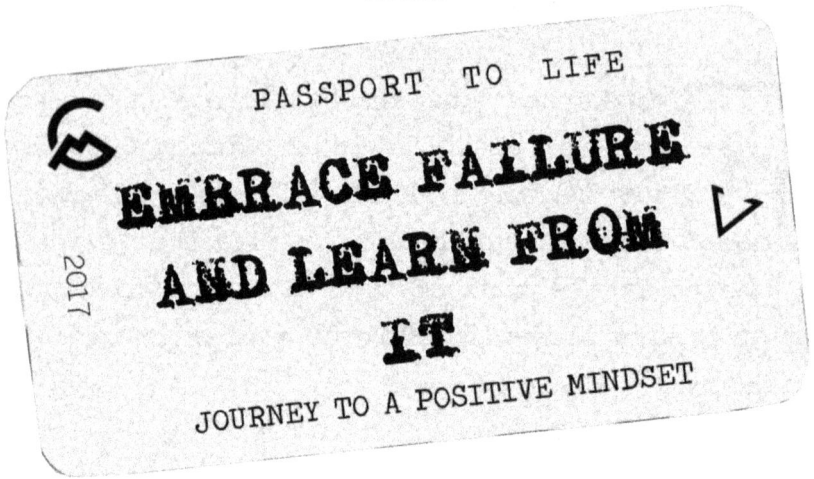

Failure is the FOUNDATION for future SUCCESS.

A setback is a set up for a comeback!

Perseverance is the key!

EMBRACE FAILURE AND LEARN FROM IT

Most people never accomplish their goals because they give up the first time things don't go as planned. Many other people never accomplish their goals because they are too afraid to take the first step.

What we must understand is that FAILURE is a part of the process. Without failure, we will have no clue as to what success looks and feels like. Think about it: if your dreams and aspirations were so easily obtainable that all you had to do was think of them and somehow magically achieve them on your first attempt, then everyone in the world would be successful.

The challenges and the obstacles that you are faced with while trying to reach your goals and dreams are what builds character and is what makes the process all worthwhile. Most people only pay attention to the birth of an idea and the end result but constantly ignore the PROCESS in between. The process itself is the most important piece to the puzzle of success. The process will make you or break you and it will work out the way it's supposed to.

The process consists of failure, pain, sacrifice, struggle, heartbreak, hopelessness, doubt, negativity etc. The process is filled with the good, the

/EMBRACE FAILURE AND LEARN FROM IT

bad and the ugly, but if you can endure all that comes with the process, the reward of success will be that much more worth it. Perseverance is the key!

11.

MAINTAIN A POSITIVE OUT LOOK

JOURNEY TO A POSITIVE MINDSET

2017

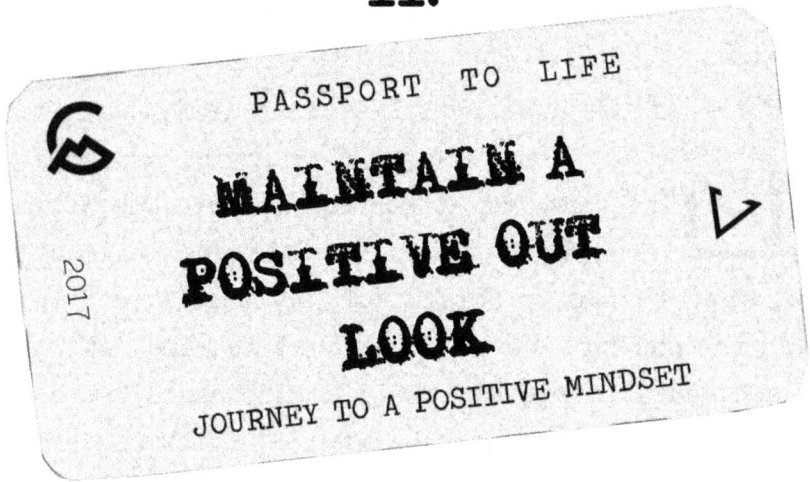

Life does not always go the way we plan it, but it's not our plan. It's God's plan!

Roadblocks are designed to test our strength and character!

God will never put anything on us that we cannot handle.

Always look at the glass as half full, everything gets better with time!

MAINTAIN A POSITIVE OUTLOOK

Life is already filled with individuals who doubt you, so why add yourself to the list? The power of attraction is real. You attract the things you think, feel and believe. Often, when things do not go our way the first time or even the second time, we think that we were not meant to succeed at whatever it may be that we're trying to accomplish. Truthfully, in most cases, all we need to do is take a step back to reassess the situation and take a different approach.

Sometimes we are too close to a situation that we cannot not see clearly and our judgment becomes cloudy. Sometimes things happen for a reason and that reason is often to teach us a lesson. When learning lessons, the focus is to not make the same mistake twice. The first time we can claim our ignorance. The second time is on us.

When problems (lessons) present themselves, we should always find the positive in that situation. Finding the positive in every situation that presents itself to you will help attract positive outcomes.

If you become more patient and positive and learn from life's lessons, the outcome will always be in your favor.

12.

PASSPORT TO LIFE

ALLOW ACTIONS TO SPEAK LOUDER THAN WORDS

2017

JOURNEY TO A POSITIVE MINDSET

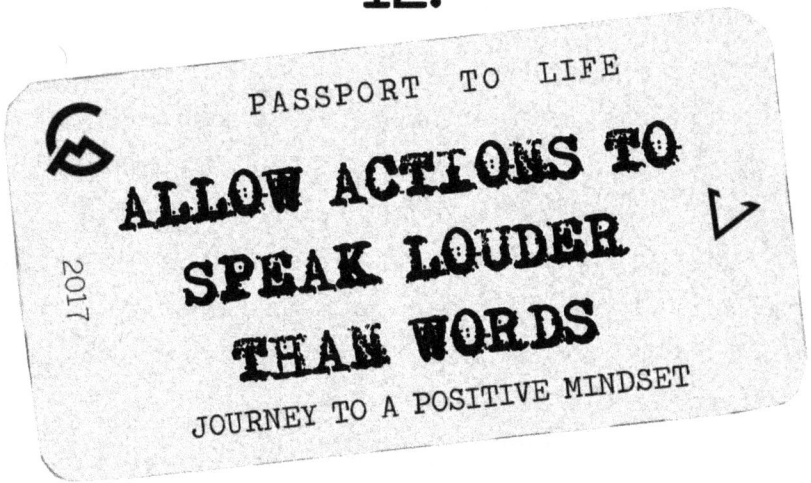

The best apology is changed behavior!

ALLOW ACTIONS TO SPEAK LOUDER THAN WORDS

Words mean nothing if the action does not follow. Society is filled with con-artists. People have a way with words and have mastered a way to say what they know you want to hear so they can get what they want from you. They may be trying to manipulate you without even realizing it.

You must "listen" to both a person's actions as well as their words and if the two don't match, then you should draw a conclusion. Trust your gut. Most times if you have a gut feeling about something or someone then there is a red flag somewhere that needs to be addressed. We often ignore the signs that are telling us everything we need to know. Why don't you believe what this person is telling you? Why don't you feel like you can trust them? It may be because someone from your past behaved the same way (said one thing and did another).

There are two types of people in the world, "say'ers" and "do'ers" and if a person is not doing what they said they were going to do, then you need to re-evaluate that person's position in your life. Don't necessarily cut this person out, but take what they say, "with a grain of salt."

13.

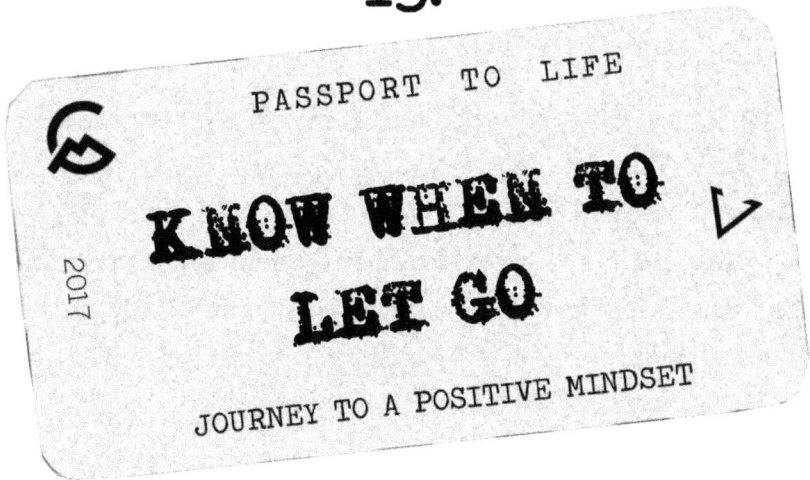

Some people are in your life for a reason, some are in your life for a season.

We have no way of knowing which one they are prior to meeting and getting to know them.

BUT, when someone shows you who they are, believe them the FIRST time!

If this person does not fit within your life's mission, it might be a good idea to eliminate them from your life or cut back on your level of involvement with them.

A ny type of good relationship is a balanced one, meaning both individuals in the relationship give and receive in approximately the same amount. Giving and receiving isn't only demonstrated in a tangible manner, it can also be time, energy, advice, empathy, respect, loyalty etc. You can usually feel it when someone is withholding more than they are offering.

If you are the person giving more in a relationship, then that relationship needs to be re-evaluated. It's OK to transition away from somebody or a situation that is doing you harm and that may not have your best interests at heart. Transitioning or separating yourself from an uneven state of affairs isn't always a bad thing. In fact, it may be all you can do about it. Complaining changes nothing; only making a change does!

Although separating yourself from a person or situation may feel bad at the time, you will later realize that life is about growth. Fear of being lonely or somehow not being good enough can keep you in an unpleasant situation longer than is necessary, but facing the possibility that it will be a healthy move can be helpful. Growth comes with changes and to grow in life, in even the smallest way, changes are necessary. If you are not ready for change, then you may not be ready for growth.

Know who you want to be and understand the changes and sacrifices that will have to be made for you to grow into the person you want to be.

DO NOT let anyone or anything stop you from becoming a better YOU!

14.

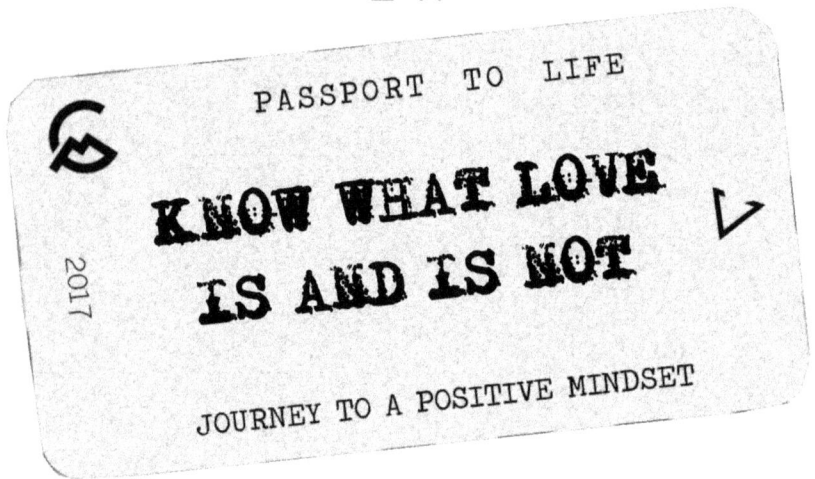

Love should NEVER hurt (Physically, Mentally or Emotionally).

If this is what "LOVE" feels like in your relationship, you may want to take a step back and re-evaluate your situation and place your energy somewhere more positive.

Love is compromising, understanding and selflessness.

Love is not easy and is hard work, but anything worth having is worth working hard for!

KNOW WHAT LOVE IS AND IS NOT

There is a fine line between tough love and abuse. Most people who abuse others (physically, mentally or emotionally) out of "love" don't realize that they are being abusive or that there is anything wrong with their behaviors. This is usually due to the environment they grew up in, and they are simply imitating the same behavior they experienced as a child. When someone sees a negative environment as the norm, it is difficult to convince them to behave in a manner other than what they have always known. They may have learned, at least subconsciously through parenting or elsewhere, that love is abusive, violent and painful. Until they mature enough to understand what loving actions and behaviors should look like, it is best to learn to identify and separate yourself from people who have this skewed vision.

Growing up in an aggressive environment is not a good enough excuse to treat someone with less respect than you would want for yourself. Break the cycle of negative behaviors and become the most positive person you can be.

Love comes in all different types of shapes, sizes and forms. Not too many people can tell you exactly what love is, but there may be quite a few people who can tell you what love is not.

Everyone loves differently and one thing you need to realize quickly is that you cannot change the way someone expresses his or her feelings. The only thing that you can change is what you accept from others.

Love is tried, love is tested, and love is true. But, as the poet Maya Angelou famously said, the moment someone shows you who they are, believe them the first time. Love has its fair share of ups and downs. However, on balance, it should be filled with happiness.

Love is caring about someone else just as much as you care for yourself. Love goes both ways. Encourage and support the person you claim to love. Think before you react or respond to situations so that your reaction will always produce the best possible outcome. Small compromises or lack thereof can make the difference between a lifetime of failed relationships or successful relationships.

15.

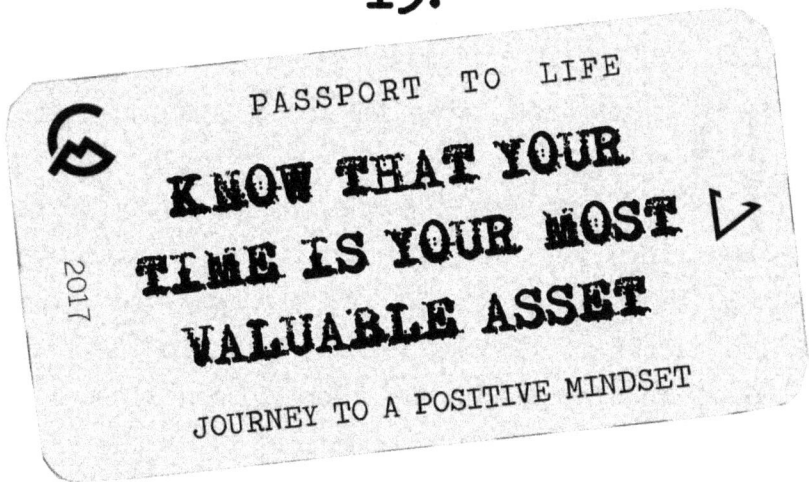

3 things to think about regarding time:

1. People make time for the things that are important to them.

2. Don't allow yourself to make other people a top priority if you are always an afterthought.

3. Treat your time like money in your bank account.

   a) Don't randomly give it away.

   b) Save some for personal usage (always get some "Me Time").

   c) Spend it on the things that matter the most to you: God, Family, Business and Friends.

KNOW THAT YOUR TIME IS YOUR MOST VALUABLE ASSET

There was a time in my life when I cared more about what other people felt or thought about me than it was worth. Meaning, it was a poor return on my investment, both in time and energy. I was the guy who always wanted to be on time, made sure I attended events, followed up with people who (most of the time) never thought about or spoke to me unless I was the one to initiate contact. These people are like "one-way streets" and I went down them the wrong way!

I would leave events tired, lose sleep, take time away from myself and other opportunities that may have been beneficial to me. It wasn't until I came to the realization that I was giving away too much of myself to people and wasn't gaining anything from it, that I realized how valuable my time was.

Spend time doing things and with people who will help you evolve. Again, life is about growth, and anything that does not help you evolve is stunting your growth.

Are you living your life to fulfill someone else's purpose? Or are you living to find and fulfill your own purpose?

The only person that has the answer to that question is you!

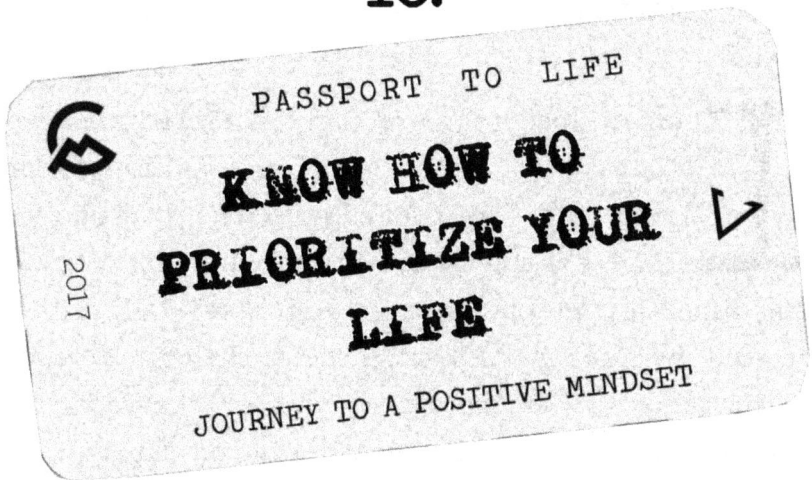

16

PASSPORT TO LIFE

KNOW HOW TO PRIORITIZE YOUR LIFE

JOURNEY TO A POSITIVE MINDSET

2017

PRIORITIES:

1. God
2. Family
3. Everything else

I often lose focus on my priorities and each time I do, I lose focus on my life. I once lived life on the edge, without structure, while at the same time neglecting what is most important. I put "everything else" in front of God and my family, allowing those things to become my top priority. Fun became my number one focus and responsibility naturally became last on the list. It's easy to confuse chaos with fun, but if a random, scattered, disorganized life is causing you pain, it's time to reorganize your life.

Once I came to the realization that "everything else" was in the wrong place on my priority list, I began to prosper. I realized that without structure and a plan, my life wasn't heading in a clear direction. It wasn't until I began to see what was truly important that my vision became clear, which allowed me to set the path for the direction I wanted my life to go in.

There is nothing wrong with wanting to have fun and enjoy life, but to truly enjoy life you must have a clear vision. To have a clear vision your priorities need to be in order. Once your priorities are in order, you can do and become anything you want to and know that you are truly on the right path to success and fulfillment.

17.

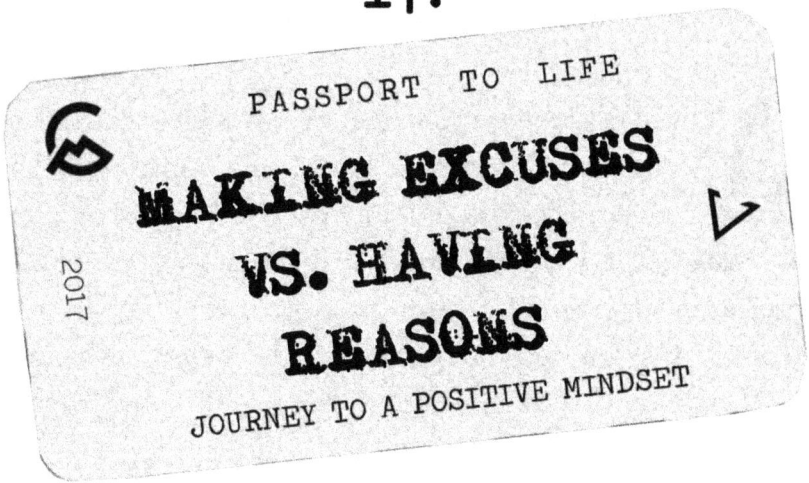

STOP using your past as an excuse to FAIL!

Instead...

Use your past as a reason to SUCCEED!

MAKING EXCUSES VS. HAVING REASONS

At almost every stage of my life there were multiple people doubting my ability to become successful. Not only that, throughout my life I have been through some extremely traumatic events. Some of the things I have gone through and the amount of doubt and negative energy that came my way was enough for me to want to just give up.

A lot of individuals attempted to crush my confidence, my spirit, and my soul. These individuals came close at times, but the one thing I knew is that I wanted to be and was going to be successful.

I chose to use those negative thoughts and views of my failures as fuel to the fire of my willingness to succeed! There was nothing I wanted more than to prove the people who doubted me wrong. At every stage of my life there were multiple obstacles and roadblocks set in my path that tried to make me to give up, panic and quit.

I decided that quitting was never an option for me and that I would always see whatever it was through to the end. I refused to let adversity be my excuse to fail! I chose to let adversity be the reason I succeeded. Whenever I felt like I wanted to give up, I simply thought about all the people who wanted me to fail and the bad life experiences I had been through, and used them as my reason to succeed! Making excuses is easy; anyone can do it. Whether they are real or imagined, turn them from the reason why you failed to the reason why you overcame.

Bad experiences make good stories and I wanted my story to be a good one in the end!

18.

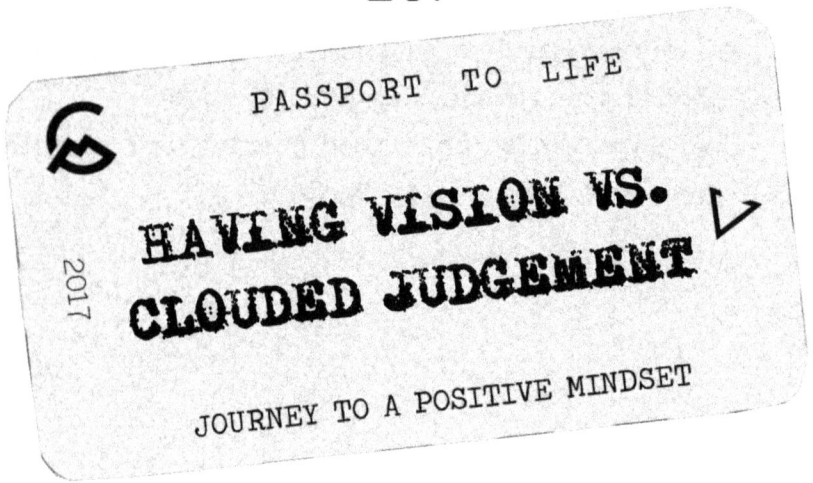

There is light at the end of the tunnel, all you need to do is keep moving!

NEVER GIVE UP!

Darkness does not last forever! Sunshine is near!

Live life and be happy!

HAVING VISION VS. CLOUDED JUDGEMENT

There are times in life when we want to just give up. Nothing seems to go our way and we cannot seem to catch a break. We are surrounded with death, financial struggles, relationship problems, health issues, etc. It seems like every time you take two steps forward, life strikes again and you end up taking ten steps backwards.

Whatever negative is happening in your life right now may seem like it's the biggest and worst life experience you have ever had to deal with and that you will never shake the dark cloud that's constantly over you. Then, somehow, things start to get better for you and you realize you are not the only person dealing with life's struggles and that there are a lot of people who are worse off than you.

You also realize that had you given up just one day prior to the day you found happiness you probably wouldn't have been able to be there to help someone else smile in his or her time of struggle. That's called "quitting before the miracle happens." Don't!

In every aspect of life there is some source of happiness near. It is up to you to find that source. The sooner you find it, the sooner you will be able to help someone else find his or hers.

/HAVING VISION VS. CLOUDED JUDGEMENT

It is OK to have cloudy days, if you understand
that clouds don't block the sunshine forever and
that the sun will be shining soon! Better yet, use the
darkness to appreciate the light and channel it into
inspiration and resolve to keep moving forward.

19.

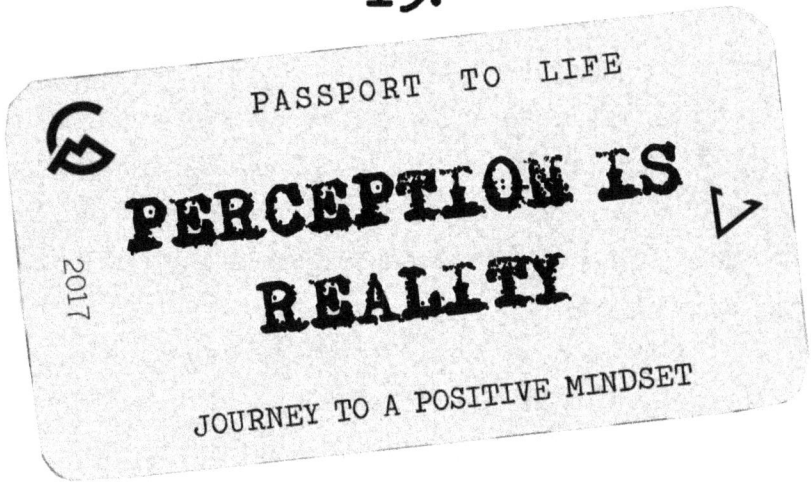

Live life in the manner you would like to be viewed.

Treat people in the manner you would like to be treated.

Love people the way you want to be loved.

Don't live life trying to clean up the negative perception people have of you. Always put your best foot forward!

You will never get a second chance to make a first impression.

PERCEPTION IS REALITY

We all have someone who has made a lasting impression on us. Whether that impression was good or bad is on the person who left it on us. No one is perfect and we all are a work in progress.

I sometimes wake up on the wrong side of the bed and leave my house in somewhat of a bad mood. I have also come across others who seemed to have the same issue. The problem is, NOBODY CARES! I don't have the right to give off my negative energy to someone who has done nothing to me. At the same time, no one has the right to give off his or her negative energy to me (especially if I have done nothing wrong to him or her).

Sometimes I can seem unapproachable when I am zoned out in thought, woke up on the wrong side of the bed or going through something personal. Either way, I have created a problem for myself, one that I have seemingly spent a lifetime trying to correct.

The point is, no one wants to get to know a person who is unpredictable. The key to fixing this problem is to always be conscious of how you come off to others and ALWAYS put your best foot forward to reduce the negative vibes you give off and instead create positive vibes.

Treat people the same way you would wanted to be treated and that will eliminate a lot of issues in the future.

20.

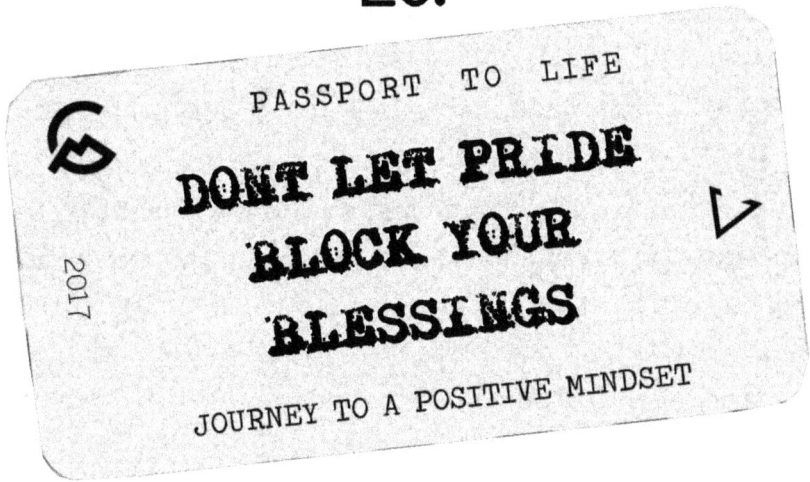

I never saw anyone win an award for having too much PRIDE.

But...

I HAVE seen many people lose a lot for having too much PRIDE.

Know when to give in.

Some battles just aren't yours to fight!

DON'T LET PRIDE BLOCK YOUR BLESSINGS

I have been in situations where I really needed someone, but this person and I had some unresolved issues from the past, possibly dating back years. Paralyzed by pride, I felt I couldn't ask them for the help I needed. The worst part was, I didn't have a problem with this person and even forgot what the unresolved issue was about. But because I knew they may have a problem with me, I refused to open my mouth in my time of need. It was like I had put up a wall around myself for no reason. The fear I had of being judged by this other person was just another form of pride.

The moment I started to communicate my feelings and emotions to resolve issues *immediately*, the less PRIDE I had. It's OK to have issues with someone if those issues get resolved one way or another. Sometimes you may have to agree to disagree with someone, but if you address the issue, everyone can move on without any negative thoughts in the back of their minds.

In life, we never know who might be the person who will save our life or give us an opportunity to become successful. Don't let pride be the reason you never got ahead.

Accept your faults, discuss the issue, resolve it respectfully and move on with life!

21.

PASSPORT TO LIFE

**COMMIT TO
BECOMING
SUCCESSFUL**

JOURNEY TO A POSITIVE MINDSET

2017

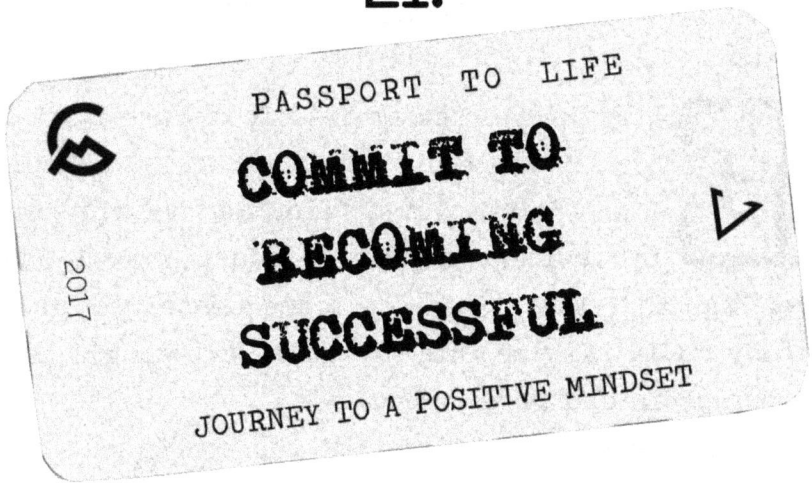

People become SUCCESSFUL the
minute they decide to be!

COMMIT TO BECOMING SUCCESSFUL

Everything I became in life was a result of what I wanted to become. When I was young I got into a lot of trouble, and it wasn't by accident, it was a choice that I made even though I knew what the consequences would be. Nobody could talk me into or out of anything; I made my own decisions, good or bad.

The moment I decided that the consequences of making bad decisions were not in my best interest, I decided to take another approach. In that approach, I decided that I wanted to be successful in life and eventually became the exact person I decided to become.

There is no single way to measure success, but if I had to define it for myself, I would say that success is simply moving in a positive direction that results in positive consequences.

Success is having tunnel vision and staying on the path that you set for yourself. Success does not come without adversity and perseverance is a must.

The moment you decide to become successful is the moment you just committed yourself to a positive lifestyle and the only way to end up successful is to stay on the right path and to overcome all obstacles that will be waiting for you on it.

Focus on your vision to success and don't let anything take you off course!

22.

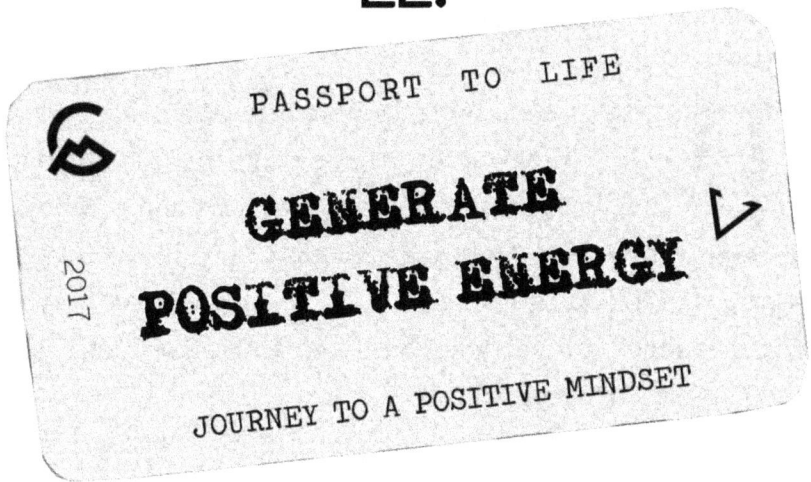

Waking up today wasn't guaranteed, so make it a good day... make it count!

Turn that negative mood into a positive one.

Watch how many blessings come your way if you just smile. Smile even when it hurts!

You're blessed!

GENERATE POSITIVE ENERGY

There are many reasons and excuses we can use for being in a negative mood. Some people will say they are being moody because they are hungry, sleepy, frustrated with school or job, relationship issues, etc. Those may be your reasons for being moody, but what are your reasons for being happy?

Everything in life happens for a reason; even the smallest things can have a huge impact. It's easy to be a negative person, but it takes much more work to be a positive person. We must practice it daily. It is worth it.

You can start by realizing that life is not promised nor is it a guarantee. You will then understand that you have a lot to smile about. Life itself is a precious gift that we often take for granted. Each day we wake up is a blessing and reason enough to smile.

There is no doubt that life is hard, but anything worth having is worth smiling for!

23.

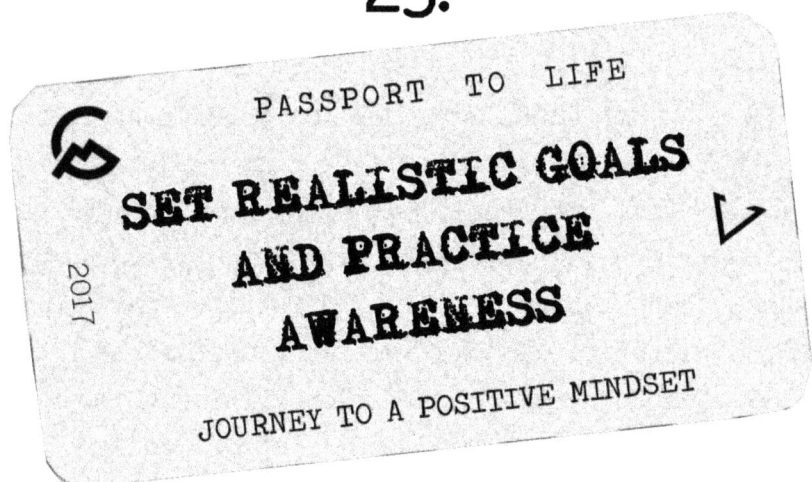

Sometimes it takes losing to realize that you are born a winner!

Stop looking too far ahead, when success is right in front of you being ignored.

Work with what you have, then turn it into what you want.

SET REALISTIC GOALS AND PRACTICE AWARENESS

All my life I have had natural talents that I was born with. I call those talents gifts. Each gift that I possess has its own lane to follow and each time I step out of that lane, I lose. It took me years to realize that all my life I was naturally blessed with the tools/gifts I needed to be successful and that if I honored them and paid attention to my path, I could utilize them almost effortlessly.

It wasn't until I started to fail at the things that I wasn't naturally gifted in did I see that, for most of my life, I had been seeking something outside of myself that I had within me all along. I just wasn't mature enough at those times to understand the difference between being gifted at something and being good at something.

I knew that I would be good at anything I set my mind to, so I ignored the natural gifts that I was given. Once I began to fail at the things I was "good" at, I started to focus on the things I was gifted at, and began to succeed more than ever before.

A successful life begins with knowing and understanding who you are as well as what your gifts are. Once you have mastered those items, there is no stopping you from winning!

24.

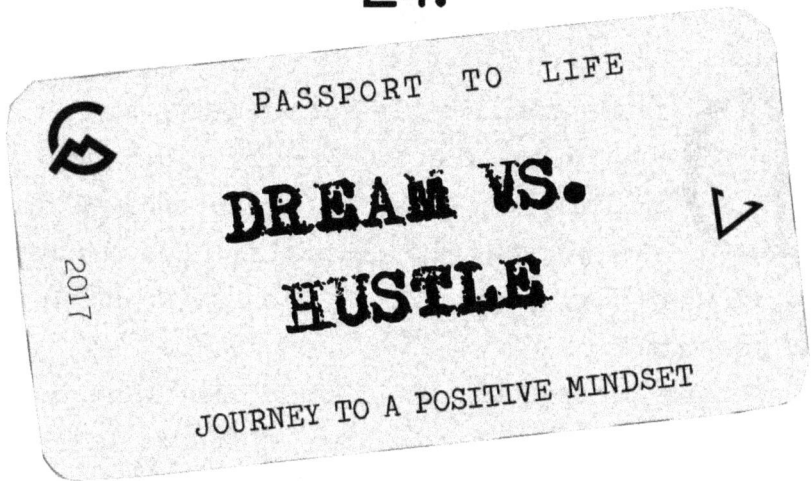

It costs nothing to dream. Hustle and sacrifice comes with a price tag.

Know that your dream is worth it and make it your reality.

Anybody can DREAM, but until you hustle to make it a REALITY, all it will ever be is a DREAM!

DREAM VS. HUSTLE

Dreams are like the spark from a match. The hustle is like the lighter fluid used to ignite the flame. The flame created from the spark by the lighter fluid is the reality of what that dream will become if the hustle is put towards it.

Many people talk about what they want to do, but not everyone puts forth the effort it takes to make their desires a reality. So in actuality, they are just all talk no action.

Dreams are just dreams until action and effort are put behind them to bring the dream to fruition. Doing research, networking and putting yourself in position to meet the opportunity you dreamed of is all a part of the hustle.

You must have a plan of action before you can turn your dream into a reality. I am a firm believer of if you fail to plan, then you plan to fail.

All success stories started with a dream. It was the hustle that made the dream come true!

25.

PASSPORT TO LIFE

STOP TRYING TO BE PERFECT

JOURNEY TO A POSITIVE MINDSET

2017

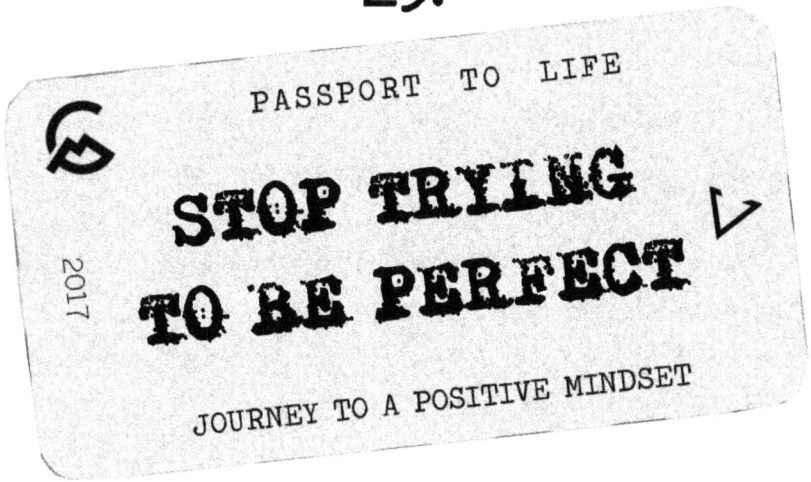

You don't have to be PERFECT!
You just have to be YOURSELF!

STOP TRYING TO BE PERFECT

We often spend so much of our time planning and strategizing to be the perfect person or come up with the perfect idea that we forget about what got us where we are today in the first place, and that is being ourselves. It's OK to prepare and to be strategic, but there is also something called "over planning and over strategizing," otherwise known as "Analysis Paralysis."

The main thing we all want to do in life is impress people and that is perfectly natural, but everyone will learn that being yourself is ultimately the only way you leave your thumbprint on the world. Each of us has something unique to offer and most of the time, that is the very reason someone might gain interest in us.

We all have something or someone that inspires us, but there comes a time when we must become comfortable with who we are so we can bring out the best in ourselves. You can only be the best version of yourself. You cannot be the best version of someone else because you are not that person and ultimately you will not be authentic. A lot of pain comes from trying to be someone you're not.

Spend more time BEING the person you are meant to be and less time planning on how to become that person.

26.

PASSPORT TO LIFE

NEVER FEEL SORRY FOR YOURSELF

2017

JOURNEY TO A POSITIVE MINDSET

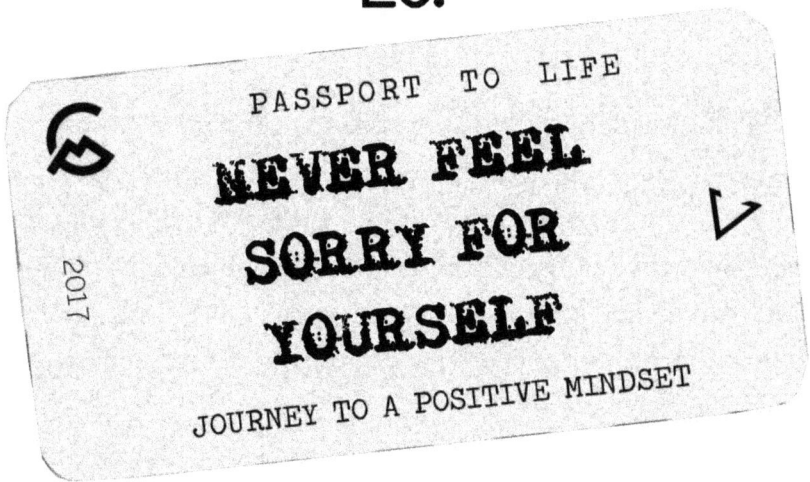

The worst part about being strong is nobody ever asks if you're OK.

The best part about it is, they don't have to!

NEVER FEEL SORRY FOR YOURSELF

I used to have a problem with the fact that not a lot of people ever checked up on me and the only time I ever heard from some people is when I reached out to them to check on them. Those thoughts came with frustration and resentment for some and complete disappointment for others.

Then I came to the realization that my feelings and emotions were just that and that they were not going to change the way others interact with me or view me. If I had a problem I needed to talk about, it was up to me to do so. The same applies to other people.

I came to the realization that regardless of what I go through in life, ultimately coming up with the solution falls on my shoulders. I may not be able to solve all my problems on my own, but I am strong enough to know when I do have a problem and how to focus on a solution to resolve it.

Dealing with life's adversity and overcoming life's obstacles builds character and strength that cannot be taken away by a single person or situation. Some of the best characteristics a person can have are a sound mind and a strong spirit to be able to encourage others.

Nobody ever said that life would be easy. God never said it would be a smooth flight, he just promised a safe landing.

27

PASSPORT TO LIFE

ALWAYS BE PREPARED

2017

JOURNEY TO A POSITIVE MINDSET

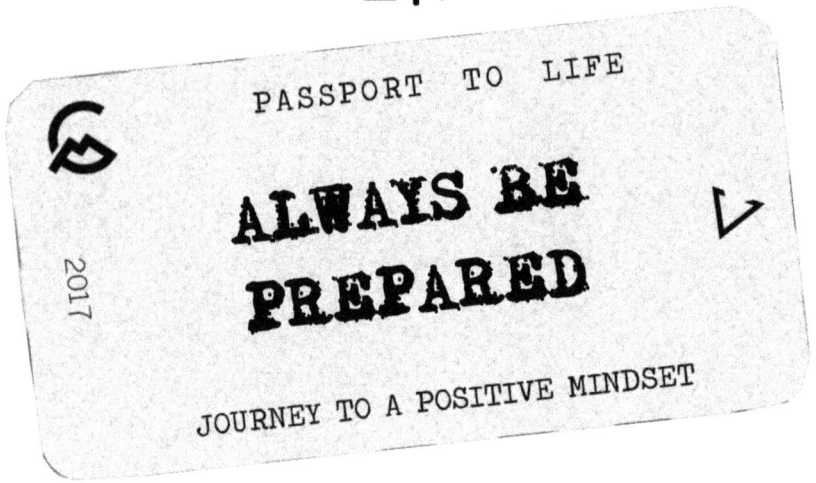

To be the BEST, you must be able to handle the WORST!

ALWAYS BE PREPARED

After experiencing traumatic events and many "bad to even worse" situations you can sometimes get in a space of hopelessness. In having those feelings of hopelessness, you almost give up on life and feel that your life will never get better or that the situation you are in or faced with is all that there will ever be.

But then you must think back to what you prayed for, what you asked God for and what you dreamed of. Then you must ask yourself if you are really prepared for the greatness that you have wanted your entire life. You must ask yourself if there's a purpose behind all that you have been through.

You should always realize that if God brought you to it, he will get you through it. Everything that happens to you and everyone else is for a reason; you just need to trust the process.

Do you expect to be the best if you haven't gone through any difficulties? Do you expect greatness to be handed to you? Or do you plan to earn it?

To earn greatness, you must go through the process and trust that you will come out on top. You should now be prepared for the worst because you have been through the worst. If the world is going to be given to you, you must be prepared to deal with everything that comes with it.

PART TWO:

HOW TO SET
EFFECTIVE GOALS

HOW DO WE SET EFFECTIVE GOALS?

Anybody can set goals, but not everyone can set *effective* goals. The problem most of us have with setting goals is that we usually randomly set goals without planning on how to reach them. Another problem most of us have with setting goals is that we do not fully understand the purpose and the process of setting goals.

Goal setting is a personal commitment to a desired achievement. The purpose of setting goals is to hold ourselves accountable, keep us focused and on the right track to accomplish our desired achievement. The process requires us to have a full understanding of ourselves and the accomplishments we want to achieve. The process for setting goals is outlined in detail below.

THE PROCESS

In understanding the process of setting effective goals, we must understand that a person who fails to plan, plans to fail. To plan effectively, there are a few steps involved in setting goals for your journey to a positive mindset.

Step 1
Create a personal mission statement:

We must start off by creating a personal mission statement. This will help us to clearly understand who we are, our passion and our purpose.

What is a personal mission statement? A personal mission statement is a short descriptive paragraph about who we are and what we stand for. A personal mission statement provides clarity and gives us a sense of purpose. It defines who we are and how we will live.

Creating a personal mission statement allows us to set goals that are aligned with our life's mission. This helps with reducing distractions and keeps us focused on what's important.

Example

"My gift and desire for helping young people overcome their obstacles makes good use of my own life experience as well as fulfills my goal of giving back to those who are less fortunate. I firmly believe that God has made me uniquely qualified to help by teaching me hard lessons, but it is up to me to maintain a positive outlook conducive to sharing my blessings with my community."

Step 2
Create a S.M.A.R.T Goal:

We must set Specific, Measurable, Achievable, Relevant and Time Sensitive (S.M.A.R.T) goals to effectively evaluate ourselves through the process.

What is a S.M.A.R.T Goal? S.M.A.R.T is an acronym that we can use to guide our goal setting.

- **Specific** (simple, sensible, significant)
- **Measurable** (meaningful, motivating)
- **Achievable** (agreed, attainable)
- **Relevant** (reasonable, realistic and resourced, results-based)
- **Time Bound** (time-based, time limited, time/cost limited, timely, time-sensitive)

Setting effective goals requires us to first understand what S.M.A.R.T goals are. The breakdown of S.M.A.R.T goals are as follows:

Specific

Our goal should be clear and specific, otherwise we won't be able to focus on our task or feel motivated to achieve it.

There are 5 W questions that need to be answered while writing a specific goal. Those 5 W's are:

1. *What* do I want to accomplish?
2. *Why* is this goal important?
3. *Who* is involved?
4. *Where* is it located?
5. *Which* resources or limits are involved?

Example

You are a sales consultant and your plan is to

The first known use of the acronym S.M.A.R.T. occurs in the November 1981 issue of *Management Review* by George T. Doran. Step 2 above and on the pages to follow is taken from Robert S. Rubin's article originally published by *The Society for Industrial and Organizational Psychology* available at https://www.mindtools.com/pages/article/smart-goals.htm

become Director of Sales. A specific goal could be, "I want to gain the skills and experience necessary to become the Director of Sales within my organization, so that I can build my career and lead a successful sales team."

Measurable

It is important to have measurable goals, so that we can track our progress and stay motivated. Assessing our progress helps us to stay focused, meet our deadlines, and adds the excitement of getting closer to achieving our goals!

A measurable goal should address questions such as:

- How much?
- How many?
- How will I know when it is accomplished?

Example

You might measure your goal of acquiring the skills to become Director of Sales by determining that you will have completed the necessary training courses and gained the relevant experience within five years' time.

Achievable

Our goal also needs to be realistic and attainable to be achievable. In other words, it should stretch our abilities, but still remain possible. When we set an achievable goal, we may be able to identify previously overlooked opportunities or resources that can bring us closer to achieving it.

An achievable goal will usually answer questions such as:

- How can I accomplish this goal?
- How realistic is the goal, based on other constraints, such as financial factors?

Example

You might need to ask yourself whether developing the skills required to become Director of Sales is realistic, based on your existing experience and qualifications. For example, do you have the time to complete the required training effectively? Are the necessary resources available to you? Can you afford to do it?

Tip:

Try not to set goals that someone else has power over. For example, "Get that promotion!" depends on who else applies, and ultimately depends on the recruiter's decision. That way, you can avoid failing at achieving your goal due to a reason beyond your control. But "Get the experience and training that I need to be considered for that promotion *IS* entirely up to you.

Relevant

This step is about ensuring that our goal matters to us, and that it also aligns with other relevant goals. We all need support and assistance in achieving our goals, but it's important to retain control over them. So, we must make sure that our plans drive everyone forward, but that we're still responsible for achieving our own goals.

A relevant goal can answer "yes" to these questions:

- Does this seem worthwhile?
- Is this the right time?
- Does this match our other efforts/needs?
- Am I the right person to reach this goal?
- Is it applicable in the current socio-economic environment?

Example:

You might want to gain the skills to become Director of Sales within your organization, but is it the right time to undertake the required training, or work toward additional qualifications? Are you sure that you're the right person for the Director of Sales role? Or do you suffer from "wishful thinking," believing you can do anything that anyone else can do as well as they can? Have you considered your spouse's goals? For example, if you want to start a family, would completing training in your free time make this more difficult?

Time-bound

Every goal needs a target date, so that we have a deadline to focus on and something to work toward. This part of the S.M.A.R.T goal criteria helps to prevent everyday tasks from taking priority over our long-term goals.

A time-bound goal will usually answer these questions:

- When?
- What can I do six months from now?
- What can I do six weeks from now?
- What can I do today?

Example:

Gaining the skills to become Director of Sales may require additional training or experience, as mentioned earlier. How long will it take you to acquire these skills? Do you need further training, so that you're eligible for certain exams or qualifications? It's important to give yourself a realistic timeframe for accomplishing the smaller goals that are necessary to achieving your final objective.

Step 3

Actively pursue your goal:

The only way to accomplish a goal is to actively pursue it. Often, we set goals for the sake of setting them and never put any effort or action into accomplishing them.

It has become normal for us to set goals because they sound good or because we truly want to accomplish them, but we are not always motivated to put forth any actions or efforts to accomplish them or even know where to start, so we fail for not having tried.

The problem is, we set goals and never act on them and that same goal lingers for months and years without ever being accomplished or ever even thought of again. We are so used to procrastinating that it becomes a part of our plan. What I mean by that is, we act more on procrastinating than we act on putting forth an effort to actually reaching our goals.

In understanding that we must actively pursue our goals, we know that it takes actual effort on our behalf to reach a successful outcome. Actively pursuing our goals means that we should be physically doing something towards our goals daily.

Step 4

Manage performance:

We must manage our performance daily, weekly and monthly to determine the progress that we are making towards our goal. Otherwise we may fall back into a cluttered mindset and not accomplish the things that need to be accomplished to get you closer to your goal.

Managing our performance requires us to evaluate and review each action needed to be taken daily, weekly or monthly to reach our goals. Evaluating your progress consists of Start Dates and Target Dates, asking yourself if you have accomplished the goals you set out to, and understanding the lessons that were learned from the process.

Your goal is the start, your objective is the outcome, and your actions is the process. To get the desired outcome, you must manage your performance each step of the way.

PART THREE:

ACTION PLANS
(GOAL SETTING)

ACTION PLAN

The purpose of the action plan/goal setting section is to allow you to set goals and strategically plan the best actions to take to accomplish your goals.

Focusing on your strengths and maintaining a positive mindset will allow you to become the best person you can be.

Each Action Plan will consist of a Goal, Objective and three Actions that will help you accomplish your goal.

These terms can be defined as follows:

Goal:

A goal is a desired result that a person plans and commits to achieve.

Objective:

An objective is something that a person's efforts or actions are intended to attain or accomplish; purpose; goal; target.

Action:

An action is the process of doing something, typically to achieve an aim.

ACTION PLAN (Example #1)

Personal: __X__ **Business:** _____ **Social:** _____
Relationship: _____ **Health:** _____

Goal: *(what do you want to accomplish?)*

"I would like to speak and be kind to my peers and control my angry and aggressive attitude."

Objective: *(your purpose for setting this goal is to...)*

"I would like to minimize the amount of rude and disrespectful interactions I have with my peers from 5 times a day to 1 time a day over the next 90 days."

Action 1: *(specific actions that will help you accomplish your goal)*

"I will practice listening to my peers completely before speaking or inserting my opinions."

Action 2: *(specific actions that will help you accomplish your goal)*

"I will speak only positive words and compliment a minimum of 10 people a day to improve my positive interaction with my peers."

Action 3: *(specific actions that will help you accomplish your goal)*

"I will practice smiling daily while in deep thought to improve my external appearance."

Goal Start Date:

Month: __Jan___ Day: ___1___ Year: __2016___

Goal Target Date:

Month: __April___ Day: ___1___ Year: __2016___

Goal accomplished?

___X___ Yes   _____ No

Explain:

"I was able to accomplish my goal consistently for 60 of the 90 days and created better relationships with my peers."

Lesson Learned:

"A lot of my failed relationships were a result of my negative attitude and perception."

ACTION PLAN (Example #2)

Personal: ____ **Business:** __X__ Social: _____
Relationship: _____ Health: _____

Goal: *(what do you want to accomplish?)*

"I would like to get a job promotion and a pay raise."

Objective: *(your purpose for setting this goal is to...)*

"I will increase my productivity by 50% and work overtime 5 days a week over the next 6 to 8 months."

Action 1: *(specific actions that will help you accomplish your goal)*

"I will dedicate 1 hour a day to marketing and contacting potential clients to increase sales and productivity for the company."

Action 2: *(specific actions that will help you accomplish your goal)*

"I will arrive at work 1 hour early and leave work 1 hour late daily, Monday through Friday."

Action 3: *(specific actions that will help you accomplish your goal)*

"I will take and pass the exam in August to become certified so that I can get a job promotion as well as a pay raise."

Evaluation

Goal Start Date:
Month: __Jan__ Day: __1__ Year: __2016__

Goal Target Date:
Month: __September__ Day: __1__ Year: __2016__

Goal accomplished?
__X__ Yes _____ No

Explain:
"I was able to accomplish my goal and successfully completed all three action plans in order to be a good candidate for a job promotion and pay raise."

Lesson Learned:
"With structure and a plan, I can accomplish anything I set my mind to."

ACTION PLAN #1

Personal: _____ Business: _____ Social: _____
Relationship: _____ Health: _____

Goal: *(what do you want to accomplish?)*

_____
_____
_____
_____

Objective: *(your purpose for setting this goal is to...)*

_____
_____
_____
_____

Action 1: *(specific actions that will help you accomplish your goal)*

_____
_____
_____
_____
_____

Action 2: *(specific actions that will help you accomplish your goal)*

_____
_____
_____

Action 3: *(specific actions that will help you accomplish your goal)*

Evaluation

Goal Start Date:

Month: _____ Day: _____ Year: _____

Goal Target Date:

Month: _____ Day: _____ Year: _____

Goal accomplished?

_____ Yes   _____ No

Explain:

Lesson Learned:

_____
_____
_____
_____
_____
_____
_____
_____
_____
_____
_____
_____

ACTION PLAN #2

Personal: _____ Business: _____ Social: _____
Relationship: _____ Health: _____

Goal: *(what do you want to accomplish?)*

_____
_____
_____
_____

Objective: *(your purpose for setting this goal is to...)*

_____
_____
_____
_____

Action 1: *(specific actions that will help you accomplish your goal)*

_____
_____
_____
_____
_____
_____

Action 2: *(specific actions that will help you accomplish your goal)*

_____
_____
_____

_____
_____
_____

Action 3: *(specific actions that will help you accom-*
plish your goal)

_____
_____
_____
_____
_____
_____

Evaluation

Goal Start Date:

    Month: _____ Day: _____ Year: _____

Goal Target Date:

    Month: _____ Day: _____ Year: _____

Goal accomplished?

    _____ Yes   _____ No

Explain:

_____
_____
_____
_____
_____
_____

Lesson Learned:

ACTION PLAN #3

Personal: _____ Business: _____ Social: _____
Relationship: _____ Health: _____

Goal: *(what do you want to accomplish?)*

_____
_____
_____
_____

Objective: *(your purpose for setting this goal is to...)*

_____
_____
_____
_____

Action 1: *(specific actions that will help you accomplish your goal)*

_____
_____
_____
_____
_____
_____

Action 2: *(specific actions that will help you accomplish your goal)*

_____
_____
_____

_____
_____
_____

Action 3: *(specific actions that will help you accomplish your goal)*

_____
_____
_____
_____
_____
_____

Evaluation

Goal Start Date:

Month: _____ Day: _____ Year: _____

Goal Target Date:

Month: _____ Day: _____ Year: _____

Goal accomplished?

_____ Yes   _____ No

Explain:

_____
_____
_____
_____
_____
_____

Lesson Learned:

ACTION PLAN #4

Personal: _____ Business: _____ Social: _____
Relationship: _____ Health: _____

Goal: *(what do you want to accomplish?)*

_____
_____
_____
_____

Objective: *(your purpose for setting this goal is to...)*

_____
_____
_____
_____

Action 1: *(specific actions that will help you accomplish your goal)*

_____
_____
_____
_____
_____
_____

Action 2: *(specific actions that will help you accomplish your goal)*

_____
_____
_____

_____
_____
_____

Action 3: *(specific actions that will help you accomplish your goal)*

_____
_____
_____
_____
_____
_____

Evaluation

Goal Start Date:

    Month: _____ Day: _____ Year: _____

Goal Target Date:

    Month: _____ Day: _____ Year: _____

Goal accomplished?

    _____ Yes   _____ No

Explain:

_____
_____
_____
_____
_____
_____

Lesson Learned:

ACTION PLAN #5

Personal: _____ Business: _____ Social: _____
Relationship: _____ Health: _____

Goal: *(what do you want to accomplish?)*

_____
_____
_____
_____

Objective: *(your purpose for setting this goal is to...)*

_____
_____
_____
_____

Action 1: *(specific actions that will help you accomplish your goal)*

_____
_____
_____
_____
_____
_____

Action 2: *(specific actions that will help you accomplish your goal)*

_____
_____
_____

Action 3: *(specific actions that will help you accomplish your goal)*

Evaluation

Goal Start Date:

Month: _____ Day: _____ Year: _____

Goal Target Date:

Month: _____ Day: _____ Year: _____

Goal accomplished?

_____ Yes   _____ No

Explain:

Lesson Learned:

_____

_____

_____

_____

_____

_____

_____

_____

_____

_____

_____

_____

ACTION PLAN #6

Personal: _____ Business: _____ Social: _____
Relationship: _____ Health: _____

Goal: *(what do you want to accomplish?)*

_____
_____
_____
_____

Objective: *(your purpose for setting this goal is to...)*

_____
_____
_____
_____

Action 1: *(specific actions that will help you accomplish your goal)*

_____
_____
_____
_____
_____
_____

Action 2: *(specific actions that will help you accomplish your goal)*

_____
_____
_____

Action 3: *(specific actions that will help you accomplish your goal)*

Evaluation

Goal Start Date:

    Month: _____ Day: _____ Year: _____

Goal Target Date:

    Month: _____ Day: _____ Year: _____

Goal accomplished?

    _____ Yes   _____ No

Explain:

Lesson Learned:

_____
_____
_____
_____
_____
_____
_____
_____
_____
_____
_____
_____
_____

ACTION PLAN #7

Personal: _____ Business: _____ Social: _____
Relationship: _____ Health: _____

Goal: *(what do you want to accomplish?)*

_____
_____
_____
_____

Objective: *(your purpose for setting this goal is to...)*

_____
_____
_____
_____

Action 1: *(specific actions that will help you accomplish your goal)*

_____
_____
_____
_____
_____
_____

Action 2: *(specific actions that will help you accomplish your goal)*

_____
_____
_____

_____

_____

Action 3: *(specific actions that will help you accomplish your goal)*

_____

_____

_____

_____

_____

_____

Evaluation

Goal Start Date:

    Month: _____ Day: _____ Year: _____

Goal Target Date:

    Month: _____ Day: _____ Year: _____

Goal accomplished?

    _____ Yes   _____ No

    Explain:

_____

_____

_____

_____

_____

_____

Lesson Learned:

_____
_____
_____
_____
_____
_____
_____
_____
_____
_____
_____
_____
_____

ACTION PLAN #8

Personal: _____ Business: _____ Social: _____
Relationship: _____ Health: _____

Goal: *(what do you want to accomplish?)*

_____
_____
_____
_____

Objective: *(your purpose for setting this goal is to...)*

_____
_____
_____
_____

Action 1: *(specific actions that will help you accomplish your goal)*

_____
_____
_____
_____
_____
_____

Action 2: *(specific actions that will help you accomplish your goal)*

_____
_____
_____

Action 3: *(specific actions that will help you accomplish your goal)*

Evaluation

Goal Start Date:

  Month: _____ Day: _____ Year: _____

Goal Target Date:

  Month: _____ Day: _____ Year: _____

Goal accomplished?

  _____ Yes   _____ No

Explain:

Lesson Learned:

ACTION PLAN #9

Personal: _____ Business: _____ Social: _____
Relationship: _____ Health: _____

Goal: *(what do you want to accomplish?)*

_____
_____
_____
_____

Objective: *(your purpose for setting this goal is to...)*

_____
_____
_____
_____

Action 1: *(specific actions that will help you accomplish your goal)*

_____
_____
_____
_____
_____
_____

Action 2: *(specific actions that will help you accomplish your goal)*

_____
_____
_____

_____

_____

Action 3: *(specific actions that will help you accomplish your goal)*

_____

_____

_____

_____

_____

_____

Evaluation

Goal Start Date:

Month: _____ Day: _____ Year: _____

Goal Target Date:

Month: _____ Day: _____ Year: _____

Goal accomplished?

_____ Yes   _____ No

Explain:

_____

_____

_____

_____

_____

_____

Lesson Learned:

_____
_____
_____
_____
_____
_____
_____
_____
_____
_____
_____
_____

ACTION PLAN #10

Personal: _____ Business: _____ Social: _____
Relationship: _____ Health: _____

Goal: (what do you want to accomplish?)

_____
_____
_____
_____

Objective: (your purpose for setting this goal is to...)

_____
_____
_____
_____

Action 1: (specific actions that will help you accomplish your goal)

_____
_____
_____
_____
_____
_____

Action 2: (specific actions that will help you accomplish your goal)

_____
_____
_____

Action 3: *(specific actions that will help you accomplish your goal)*

Evaluation

Goal Start Date:

Month: _____ Day: _____ Year: _____

Goal Target Date:

Month: _____ Day: _____ Year: _____

Goal accomplished?

_____ Yes   _____ No

Explain:

Lesson Learned:

ACTION PLAN #11

Personal: _____ Business: _____ Social: _____
Relationship: _____ Health: _____

Goal: *(what do you want to accomplish?)*

_____
_____
_____
_____

Objective: *(your purpose for setting this goal is to...)*

_____
_____
_____
_____

Action 1: *(specific actions that will help you accomplish your goal)*

_____
_____
_____
_____
_____

Action 2: *(specific actions that will help you accomplish your goal)*

_____
_____
_____

_____

_____

Action 3: *(specific actions that will help you accomplish your goal)*

_____

_____

_____

_____

_____

_____

Evaluation

Goal Start Date:

Month: _____ Day: _____ Year: _____

Goal Target Date:

Month: _____ Day: _____ Year: _____

Goal accomplished?

_____ Yes   _____ No

Explain:

_____

_____

_____

_____

_____

_____

Lesson Learned:

_____
_____
_____
_____
_____
_____
_____
_____
_____
_____
_____
_____
_____
_____

ACTION PLAN #12

Personal: _____ Business: _____ Social: _____
Relationship: _____ Health: _____

Goal: *(what do you want to accomplish?)*

_____
_____
_____
_____

Objective: *(your purpose for setting this goal is to…)*

_____
_____
_____
_____

Action 1: *(specific actions that will help you accomplish your goal)*

_____
_____
_____
_____
_____
_____

Action 2: *(specific actions that will help you accomplish your goal)*

_____
_____
_____

_____

_____

_____

Action 3: *(specific actions that will help you accom-plish your goal)*

_____

_____

_____

_____

_____

_____

Evaluation

Goal Start Date:

Month: _____ Day: _____ Year: _____

Goal Target Date:

Month: _____ Day: _____ Year: _____

Goal accomplished?

_____ Yes   _____ No

Explain:

_____

_____

_____

_____

_____

_____

Lesson Learned: